The
Adult Lovers Shadow Tarot & Oracle

Guide Book & Printable 78 Card Deck

Artwork & Concept
By
A.R. Jones

Disclaimer-

I in no way take responsibility for the messages and energy the Universe sends you to decipher, Nor how you interpret it. Nor am I responsible for any Karma you have or acquire. This material is of an adult nature and not for those under 18 years of age.

It is my hope you shall find the answers you're looking for.

Please do keep in mind that these insights should be regarded as a means to assess the overall and immediate energy of a situation; tarot is about direction and the future isn't written in stone. The Energy is always in flux and changes as your decisions change and the Universal Energy changes.

The Adult Lovers Shadow Tarot & Oracle

Guide Book & Printable 78 Card Deck

The Adult Lovers Shadow Tarot & Oracle

The Adult Shadow Lovers Tarot is a hand drawn Combined Tarot & Oracle Deck. Each card is unique. Each image is hand drawn and colored to reflect a dream like landscape or place with the positions based off of the kama sutra. Each card has been designed with Tarot, Oracle & Numerology in mind, combining all three in each card. This particular deck has the traditional Tarot on one side and blank on the back.. This Deck is designed to read the Romantic energies of life and will help you to better understand your situation and how it will impact you.

Due to the adult imagery of the deck and the difficulty printing it I have decided to include a PDF link to print the deck in Sm size and Poker size so that you shall be able to print the deck for your personal use as many times as you like with the purchase of the Guide Book.

The link will include-

-Poker size Printable deck of 78 cards (11 Sheets)

-Front Card template

Color Printing can be done at any local shop near you on heavy cardstock and is durable for ($5-9.00).

Remember to consider

-The Basic Meaning of each Tarot card

-The image itself

-The Oracle Word

-The card Number & Spiritual Meaning

- The entire story the Cards are trying to tell you

0 The Fool-Air- A Blessing

Self reflection. The beginning of your quest for knowledge.New beginnings, optimism, trust in life. Reconsidering who you are and where you're going. Identity and self discovery. Being put on a new path, Reaping what you sow, Discovery of truth.

Upright: innocence, new beginnings, free spirit,

Reversed: recklessness, taken advantage of, inconsideration

In Love: Losing virginity. A new lover who takes you to new levels of sexuality and spirituality. Going beyond one's sexual experience into new areas.New or original sexual experiences. An exciting or unpredictable lover.

0. God is talking to you. When you see a zero, it's a sign of the endless circle of Omega without beginning or end. God is trying to get your attention with a word of reassurance or Divine guidance.

1 The Magician -Mercury - Gifted

Male Energy of your mind. Knowledge through experience. Action, the power to manifest. Great skill in many things. Reaction and planning. A person of Spiritual Gifts and understanding, Strong of mind and will.

Upright: willpower, desire, creation, manifestation,

Reversed: trickery, illusions, out of touch.

In Love: Reading or writing about sex. Letters, email, texting a lover.Telephone sex.Sexting. Bisexuality. Male Energy

1. Stay positive. Everything you're thinking about right now is coming true, so be sure that you're only thinking about what you desire. Give any fears to God and the angels.

2 The High Priestess -Moon -Real-life Vs Fantasy

The female energy of your mind ,Inaction, going within, the subconscious.Rumination of all things. Logic, Emotion and Intuition. Gifted. Blessed by a higher Power, Old Soul, Deep understanding of the world and Life, Powerful and Just, Foresight and Intuition & Guides speak to them.

Upright: intuitive, unconscious, inner voice,

Reversed: lack of center, lost inner voice, repressed feelings

In Love: Fluctuations in sexual energy.Traveling long distance to meet a sexual partner.Using intercourse to explore spirituality. Renunciation of sex.Practising abstinence.

2. Everything's fine and will continue to be so. Keep believing, especially since your feelings of hope lead to more positive outcomes. The angels can buoy your faith if you'll ask for their help.

3 The Empress_-Venus - Universal Message

The ability to acknowledge ego, and understand that it serves as a teacher to protect yourself, from your self – being able to think fast, and still have loving intention. Abundance, nurturing, fertility, life in bloom! Wise is logic, mind, heart, spirit and soul.

Upright: motherhood, fertility, nature,

Reversed: dependence, smothering, emptiness, nosiness

In Love: Passionate indulgence. Sex for procreation, creativity, or with a married or status woman. Pregnancy. Partnership. Creation.

3. The ascended masters are helping you—usually this means an ascended master you feel close to or some other spiritual/religious figure.

4 The Emperor_-Aries - Affectionate

Not allowing ego to be your primary decision maker, and understanding that the only thing you will always be wearing is your soul, stable and capable..Structure, stability, rules and power. Male energy of Passion and Lust, Great purpose oe path to follow.

Upright: authority, structure, control, fatherhood,

Reversed: tyranny, rigidity, coldness

In Love: Sex with an older partner, an employer, politician, military person or status individual or that involves domination or strict rules.Dressing up. Sexuality to gain promotion. Laying down the law, or strict rules on sexuality. Advice on sex.

4. The angels are with you. They send you the number 4 to reassure you that they've heard your prayers and are helping you.

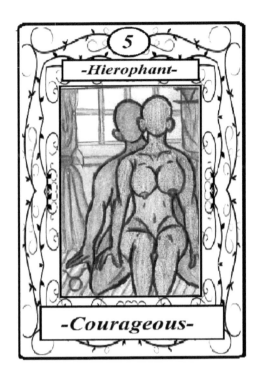

5 The Hierophant-Taurus - Courageous

Finding balance between soul and ego and world. Letting go of the need to fix everything, and understanding there is no need to interfere, you must only guide, and lead by example.Institutions, tradition, society and its rules. Be yourself and trust your Devine and Guides and intuition given to you.

Upright: tradition, conformity, morality, ethics,

Reversed: rebellion, subversiveness, new approaches

In Love: Sex within marriage or teaching an inexperienced partner, or a religious person, priest, etc.Conventional, unadventurous, perfunctory or passionless sex. Proposal of marriage.Religious advice on love and sexuality.

5. A significant change is occurring, always for the better. It's a good idea to call upon Heaven for help with life changes.

6 The Lovers -Gemini - True Love

The Lovers are not what you imagine. The card doesn't represent just a significant other, but rather – the lesson of The Lovers is to live life with love being your primary objective.Sexuality, passion, choice, uniting in a Love based relationship, Pairing. A deep connection in mind, body or spirit to a person. Equal give & Take. Hopes & Dreams, Future Planning.

Upright: partnerships, duality, union,

Reversed: loss of balance, one-sidedness, disharmony

In Love: Exploring between lovers.Lovers who are very similar in outlook, interests. Lovers who are neighbours.Writing love letters, emails, texting or phoning a lover. News about a lover. A True Connection.

6. Don't worry or obsess about material items, including money. Worry lowers the effectiveness of your prayers. Fortunately, the angels can answer your prayers if you ask them to.

7 The Chariot -Cancer - Adventurous

The Chariot represents being aware of the consequences of your actions, and not allowing sexual desires/false bravado/others, to be your guiding forces. Movement, progress, integration. Path progression and movement toward your goals and how to achieve them.

Upright: direction, control, willpower,

Reversed: lack of control, lack of direction, aggression

In Love: Dominating or controlling sex. Obsession or Sexual obsession with a partner. Lust. Long Distance.Age Gap.

7. You're on the right path, and the outcome will exceed your expectations! The number 7 is a sign that Divine magic is supporting you and opening doors of opportunity.

8 Strength -Leo - Self Love

Remembering to be a warrior inside, not a worrier ... approaching life with an open heart, and staying strong during adversity. Courage, subtle power, integration of animal self. Being your own strength and being others strength when there is a need. The courage and conviction to do what is right instead of what is easy.

Upright: inner strength, bravery, compassion, focus,

Reversed: self doubt, weakness, insecurity

In Love: A passionate love affair. Primal Urges.Sex magick or Manifesting. Taking risks. Stamina. Lots of Sex. Kinks.

8. The number 8 signifies abundance and prosperity. The endless loops in this number signify an infinite flow of money, time, ideas, or whatever else you require (especially for your life purpose).

9 The Hermit -Virgo - Dedicated

Finding appreciation for solitude, because it can serve to remind you of your true purpose. Meditation, solitude, consciousness. Reflection on one's path, deeds and goals. Rumination. Seeking answers, truth and understanding. Looking at the spider web of life. Consideration of choices.

Upright: contemplation, search for truth, inner guidance,

Reversed: loneliness, isolation, lost your way

In Love: Abstinence. A secret lover.Masturbation.

Renunciation.A secret passion or obsession for someone – secrets.

Feeling alone. Affair with a work colleague.Counselling.

9. Get to work, now! The number 9 means that you've completed all of the prerequisites to achieve your life purpose. Stop procrastinating, as it's time to start taking action steps. Even baby steps are useful.

10 The Wheel of Fortune -Jupiter - Universeal Change

The only permanence is impermanence. Fortune can change instantly, and it is important to remain grateful – always.
Cycles, Change, ups and downs. The World stops for No One, Progression of Self and Life as a Whole.

Upright: change, cycles, inevitable fate,

Reversed: no control, clinging to control, bad luck

In Love: A change in partner. A whirlwind romance. Relocation. Travel. Changes in your Relationship.

10. God wants you to hold positive thoughts about this situation, as everything is working out for your highest good. Call upon God to help you stay optimistic, as your thoughts are an influencing factor in the outcome.

11 Justice -Libra - Choices & Paths

You reap what you sow, and for every action there is a reaction and another and another in an endless web of fate. Fairness, equality, balance. We All answer to Others for our Deeds. Truth & Justice are given to all Beings, The Judge, Jury & Executioner of our Fates is US.

Upright: cause and effect, clarity, truth,

Reversed: dishonesty, unaccountability, unfairness

In Love: A legal marriage. Aesthetically pleasing or beautiful playmate. An Older partner or foreigner. The legal aspects of sexuality. Divorce. Cheating or Third Party is possible.

11. Stay positive! Your thoughts are materializing rapidly, so you want to ensure positive outcomes by focusing only on the good within yourself, others, and this situation.

12 The Hanged Man - Water - Self Sabotage

It is far better to confront your demons, and allow them to be your teachers as opposed to having them be as your corruptors and destroy you. Learn and Surrender, new perspective, enlightenment. The Universe gives us many lessons to Learn and Grow and Progress.

Upright: sacrifice, release, martyrdom,

Reversed: stalling, needless sacrifice, fear of sacrifice

In Love: Suffering in silence. Sexual submission.

An abusive relationship. Making sacrifices for a partner.

Fruitless waiting for the person to come into one's life. Loss.

12. Keep your thoughts positive about the future, as what you are thinking influences your future. This is a message to keep your faith and hope strong because these are strong determining factors right now.

13 Death -Scorpio - Beginning/Ending a Relationship

An end is just a new beginning.The end of something, change, the impermeability of all things. Reconsider with new eyes all you experience.Be open and work with the energy instead of against it. Discover your true self and be yourself.

Upright: end of cycle, beginnings, change, metamorphosis,

Reversed: fear of change, holding on, stagnation, decay

In Love: Death of a partner.An intense relationship. Sex for money or in secret places. Sexual disease.

Discovering secrets. A Secret Partner. Obsession.

13. The ascended masters (such as Jesus, Quan Yin, and so on) are with you, helping you maintain a positive outlook. The number 13 signifies that female ascended masters and goddesses are assisting you in staying positive.

14 Temperance- Sagittarius - Patience

Patience and persistence for what you're passionate about. Purification, Health, Harmony, Self Worth and Stability. Balance, moderation, being sensible. Achievement through hard work and diligence.

Upright: middle path, patience, finding meaning,

Reversed: extremes, excess, lack of balance

In Love: Sex as a higher or spiritual calling. Holiday romances, or a foreign partner. Complicated sexual relationships involving several partners. The inability to manage or cope with a relationship. Runner.

14. Lean upon the angels to help you maintain a positive outlook. This will keep your own demeanor optimistic and bright.

15 The Devil - Capricorn - Seduction

The Devil is not a "monster," but instead it is The Monster that chains you to a lower vibration because of choices made or not made, primarily for egotistical gain. Destructive patterns, addiction, giving away your power. A person of power, knowledge and great skill who is in there power and element, Skilled in mind and Spirit. Gifted, Old and Wise in Soul. The Devil is an angel who fell for Advocating for Humanity. Our inner Devils are Good & Bad. It's a Choice.

Upright: addiction, materialism, playfulness,

Reversed: freedom, release, restoring control

In Love: An intense or suffocating relationship. Bondage.A corporate or business love affair.

Desire for domination or subjugation. Being tied up.Obsession with one's Partner. A Toxic Energy.

15. As you go through changes in your life, stay positive. Your optimistic thoughts help you manifest the best outcomes with respect to these changes.

16 The Tower-Mars - Lessons & Change

A reminder to be humble and appreciate all that you have, as well as what you can have. Also, to be aware that once you get what you wish for, you must not take it for granted.Collapse of stable structures, release, sudden insight, Change of Path, Truths Revealed, Foundations need Rebuilt, The Universe is stepping in to show you something.

Upright: sudden upheaval, broken pride, disaster,

Reversed: disaster avoided, delayed disaster, fear of suffering

In Love: A dominating, violent, oppressive, abusive or disintegrating relationship.

Sex with someone in the military. Discovering shocking aspects to a partner's sexuality.

Realising a partner is not faithful.

16. Your words are magnetic affirmations that draw to you the very things you talk and think about. For this reason, the angels remind you to be aware of your words and thoughts.

17 The Star-Aquarius - Trust

To be able to see the stars, you must know the darkness, and in order to see the light, you must know that even in the light, the dark exists but is only there to cradle the stars.
Hope, calm, a good omen or a new insight into an event. Revelation and understanding.
A wish

Upright: hope, faith, rejuvenation,

Reversed: faithlessness, discouragement, insecurity

In Love: Inspirational sex. Seeing someone as a friend and a lover. Desiring a love affair with a friend or acquaintance. Cybersex.Unconventional relationships. Flirting.Finding a lover at a social event.

17. The angels applaud you for staying positive and optimistic. They say that your optimism is warranted, as your affirmative thoughts are coming true. Keep up the good work, as you're on the right path!

18 The Moon-Pisces - Hope

Masculine energy, being called to be the best "Man/ Woman" you can be. Mystery, the subconscious, dreams. Manifestation. The mysterious and unknown, a new view or path. Pay attention to the signs and details. Illusion, Powerful, Secretive, Mysterious.

Upright: unconscious, illusions, intuition,

Reversed: confusion, fear, misinterpretation

In Love: Sexual fantasies or phobias. Confusion about relationships. Fear of Infidelity.Ambiguous sexuality.

Sex-magic. Erotic Dreams. Deep Needs.

18. Your thoughts are the valve that opens and shuts your financial flow. As you stay positive, all the material

resources you need come to you easily. However, worry can stop this flow, so ask your angels to help you stay

upbeat, especially where it concerns money.

19 The Sun- Sun - Celebration

Finding balance between the day and the night, and remembering the lesson of the sun – be light, be bright, be warm, and inspire life to flourish by what you project to your surroundings.Success, happiness, all will be well. Energy is in us and all around us and is in every part of life. The Divine Higher Power.

Upright: joy, success, celebration, positivity,

Reversed: negativity, depression, sadness

In Love: A happy stable sexual relationship. Romance. Engagement. Love & Lust. Trust.

Commitment. Happy with partner. Blessed Future.

19. This is a message for you to believe in yourself and your life purpose. The angels want you to know that you are qualified and ready to follow your dreams. Stay positive, and take action without delay.

20 Judgement - Fire - Reflection

Responsibility for the past to progress in the future. Rebirth, a new phase, inner calling. A balancing of the scales, making a decision. The Universe shall judge us all by our deeds and Lessons learned. Consider your course.

Upright: reflection, reckoning, awakening,

Reversed: lack of self awareness, doubt, self loathing

In Love: Making a decisions on a relationship. Inability to deal with issues in a relationship.

Problems with timing. Not enough time for a relationship. The wrong time for a relationship, or there is never time for a relationship.

20. Your connection with the Creator is strong and clear. God asks you to fill your heart and mind with faith (ask Heaven for help in doing so if you desire). Your faith is being rewarded right now.

21 The World- Saturn - Happiness

Know yourself, and you will know the world. Know the world, and you will know yourself. Completion, wholeness, attainment, celebration of life. Divine path or choice or energy.New Cycle. Conclusion. Seeing the Big Picture.

Upright: fulfillment, harmony, completion,

Reversed: incompletion, no closure

In Love: End of a love affair. Meeting one's desire.The object of one's obsession. Anal-sex. Love affair on holiday or a foreign country. Trying New things. Intense Passion. Happy with Partner.

21. Your optimism is definitely warranted! The angels are working behind the scenes on your behalf right this very minute. You can help support the angels' work by saying positive affirmations and believing that your dream is already manifesting.

Earth & Matter

Earth is the actual physical body and therefore the most sensual and sexual Element but it goes without saying that it needs components from the other Elements in order to get sexually 'fired up.'

The Earth Signs:

Taurus, Virgo, Capricorn

Earth signs keep it real. They are the "grounded" people on the planet, the ones who bring us down to earth and remind us to start with a solid foundation. Slow and steady, these "builders" are loyal and stable, and stick by their people through hard times. On good days, they're practical; at worst, they can be materialistic or too focused on the surface of things to dig into the depths.

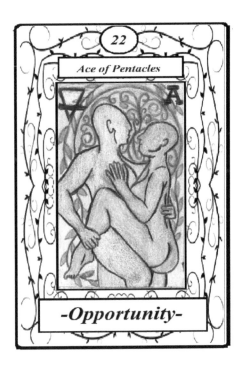

22 Ace of Pentacles - Opportunity

Upright: opportunity, prosperity, new venture,

Reversed: lost opportunity, missed chance, bad investment

In Love:Gratification

22. The angels can see the positive results of your prayers, and they want you to have patience and stay optimistic while the final details are being worked out in Heaven. This is an urgent call from the angels to "keep the faith"!

23 Two of Pentacles- Decisions

Upright: balancing decisions, priorities, adapting to change,

Reversed: loss of balance, disorganized, overwhelmed

In Love:Embarrassment

23. You are working closely with one or more ascended masters such as Jesus, Moses, the saints, or the goddesses. This is a message from your ascended master guides, who can see that the answer to your prayers is within reach. They encourage you to stay positive to ensure that you attract the best possible outcome.

24 Three of Pentacles- Give & Take

Upright: teamwork, collaboration, building,

Reversed: lack of teamwork, disorganized, group conflict

In Love: Warmth

24. Additional angels are surrounding you right now, helping you stay optimistic no matter what is going on around you. The angels know the magical power of faith, and they're releasing any negative thoughts and emotions to give you a clear path for the manifestation of your desires.

25 Four of Pentacles- Self Preservation

Upright: conservation, frugality, security,

Reversed: greediness, stinginess, possessiveness

In Love:Pleasure

25. As you go through major life changes, expect the best and your optimism will be rewarded.

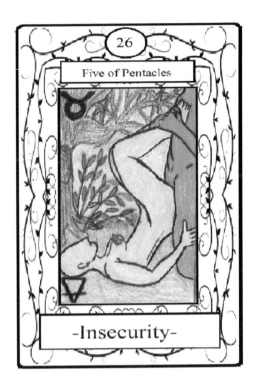

26 Five of Pentacles- Insecurity

Upright: need, poverty, insecurity,

Reversed: recovery, charity, improvement

In Love:Completeness

26. Positive affirmations help your situation improve quickly. The angels urge you to only think and speak about your desires, and not to affirm your fears, as they are just an illusion.

27 Six of Pentacles- Gifts

Upright: charity, generosity, sharing,

Reversed: strings attached, stinginess, power and domination

In Love:Boredom

27. Congratulations! Your optimism is attracting wonderful situations and relationships.
Stay positive, as this attitude is working in your favor.

28 Seven of Pentacles- Hard Work

Upright: hard work, perseverance, diligence,

Reversed: work without results, distractions, lack of rewards

In Love:Tiredness

28. Money comes to you as you keep the faith that you, your loved ones, and your beautiful life purpose are all fully supported by Heaven.

29 Eight of Pentacles- Passion & Lust

Upright: apprenticeship, passion, high standards,

Reversed: lack of passion, uninspired, no motivation

In Love:Indifference

29. Stay positive about your life purpose, and put all of your focus on being of service, utilizing your natural talents, passions, and interests. Doors are opening. for you. Just keep your faith strong.

30 Nine of Pentacles- Rewards

Upright: fruits of labor, rewards, luxury,

Reversed: reckless spending, living beyond means, false success

In Love:Domination

30. You are fully supported by God and the ascended masters. Step forward confidently in the direction of your dreams!

31 Ten of Pentacles- Your Life

Upright: legacy, culmination, inheritance,

Reversed: fleeting success, lack of stability, lack of resources

In Love: Desire

31. The ascended masters ask you to look past all earthly illusions and see the Divine perfection within you, other people, and your current situation. As you can see Divine perfection in your mind, it manifests externally in your relationships, career, health, and other life areas.

32 Page of Pentacles- Desire & Drive

Upright: ambition, desire, diligence,

Reversed: lack of commitment, greediness, laziness

In Love:Arousal

32. The ascended master Jesus reminds you to apply his affirmation about the power of faith ("With faith, all things are possible") to your own life right now.

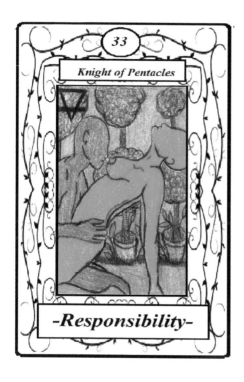

33 Knight of Pentacles- Responsibility

Upright: efficiency, hard work, responsibility,

Reversed: laziness, obsessiveness, work without reward

In Love:Discontent

33. You have a strong and clear connection with one or more ascended masters, who have answered your call and your prayers. Keep talking to them, as they're helping you with your present situation.

34 *Queen of Pentacles- Security*

Upright: practicality, creature comforts, financial security,

Reversed: self-centeredness, jealousy, smothering

In Love:Coolness

34. Your prayers are heard and answered by the angels and ascended masters, who are with you right now.

35 King of Pentacles- Prosperity

Upright: abundance, prosperity, security,

Reversed: greed, indulgence, sensuality

In Love:Fear

35. A positive change is coming about for you, with the assistance and protection of the ascended masters.

Air & Thought

Air is intellectual energy. This is the least sexual/sensual energy and it needs to be carefully grounded into the body in order to find sexual expression.

The Air Signs:

Gemini, Libra, Aquarius

Air signs are all about action, ideas, and motion—they are the "winds of change." When a strong gust hits you, you can't help but move. While some within their ranks may be true-life "airheads," others are as powerful as a gravity-defying G-force. Air signs bring everyone a breath of fresh air when things start to get stale. Like the breeze, you can't quite catch them, and you never know where they'll drop you once they sweep you up. It will almost always been an adventure, though.

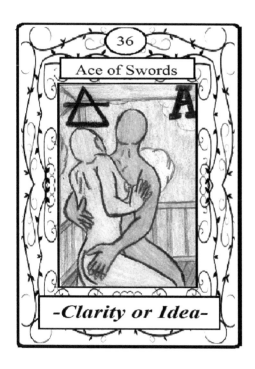

36 Ace of Swords- Clarity or Idea

Upright: breakthrough, clarity, sharp mind,

Reversed: confusion, brutality, chaos

In Love:Bonding

36. The ascended masters ask you to keep your thoughts focused on spirit, and release any material worries to them.

37 Two of Swords- Difficult Choices

Upright: difficult choices, indecision, stalemate,

Reversed: lesser of two evils, no right choice, confusion

In Love:Inviting

37. You are on the right path, and the ascended masters are encouraging and helping you along the way.

38 Three of Swords- Heartbreak or Third Party

Upright: heartbreak, suffering, grief,loss, Break up, third party, drama, lies

Reversed: recovery, forgiveness, moving on, giving up

In Love:Pinching

38. The ascended masters are helping you with your financial situation.

39 Four of Swords- Contemplation

Upright: rest, restoration, contemplation,

Reversed: restlessness, burnout, stress

In Love:Masturbateing

39. You are being helped by the ascended masters, who are strongly encouraging you to work on your life purpose right now.

40 Five of Swords- Drama

Upright: unbridled ambition, win at all costs, sneakiness,

Reversed: lingering resentment, desire to reconcile, forgiveness

In Love:Shaking things up

40. God and the angels are surrounding you with Heavenly love and protection.

41 Six of Swords- Let it Go

Upright: transition, leaving behind, moving on,

Reversed: emotional baggage, unresolved issues, resisting transition

In Love:Rolling About

41. The angels ask you to keep very positive thoughts, as everything you say and think is manifesting into form rapidly.

42 Seven of Swords- Deception

Upright: deception, trickery, tactics and strategy,

Reversed: coming clean, rethinking approach, deception

In Love:Tasting

42. The angels are urging you to keep the faith!

43 Eight of Swords- Bad Idea/Choice

Upright: imprisonment, entrapment, self-victimization,

Reversed: self acceptance, new perspective, freedom

In Love:Scratching

43. Both the angels and ascended masters are helping you right now. Spend time connecting with them in quiet meditation, and be calmed by their reassuring presence, which tells you that everything is fine.

44 Nine of Swords- UnHappy

Upright: anxiety, hopelessness, trauma,

Reversed: hope, reaching out, despair

In Love:Rubbing

44. The angels are giving you extra comfort, love, and support right now. Ask them for
help with everything, and listen to their guidance through your intuition.

45 Ten of Swords- Loss or Feeling Lost

Upright: failure, collapse, defeat,

Reversed: can't get worse, only upwards, inevitable end

In Love:Squeezing

45. The angels are helping you through a positive life change.

46 Page of Swords- Unstable

Upright: curiosity, restlessness, mental energy,

Reversed: deception, manipulation, all talk

In Love:Biting

46. The angels are saying to you: "Keep your thoughts focused upon your spiritual self and your Divine Source for everything. Give any material worries to us."

47 Knight of Swords- Acting Without Thinking

Upright: action, impulsiveness, defending beliefs,

Reversed: no direction, disregard for consequences, unpredictability

In Love: Taming

47. The angels say that you are on the right path. Keep up the good work!

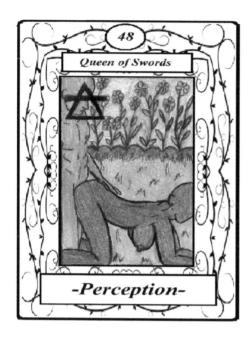

48 Queen of Swords- Perception

Upright: complexity, perceptiveness, clear mindedness,

Reversed: cold hearted, cruel, bitterness

In Love:Exploring

48. Your prayers about money have been heard and answered by the angels.

49 King of Swords- Actions & Reactions

Upright: head over heart, discipline, truth,

Reversed: manipulative, cruel, weakness

In Love:Fondling

49. The angels urge you to get to work on your major goals and life purpose without delay. Ask them to help you with ideas, courage, and motivation.

Will & Fire

Fire is raw sexual energy. It's active/yang. It is fuelled by alcohol (Fire) and sometimes aggression (also Fire) seeks sexual expression.

The Fire Signs:

Aries, Leo, Sagittarius

Like fire itself, fire signs tend to be passionate, dynamic, and temperamental. Fire can keep you warm, or it can do great destruction. While fire burns out quickly without fuel to keep it going, it can also regenerate its power from the ashes. A single spark can set off a forest fire. As a result, fire signs need to be nurtured and managed carefully.

50 Ace of Wands- Manifestation

Upright: creation, willpower, inspiration, desire,

Reversed: lack of energy, lack of passion, boredom

In Love:Union. A Birth. New Path

50. God is helping you to change your life in healthful new ways.

51 Two of Wands- Thinking Before Acting

Upright: planning, making decisions, leaving home,

Reversed: fear of change, playing safe, bad planning

In Love:Nearness

51. Keep positive thoughts about the changes you're desiring and experiencing.

52 Three of Wands- Plans or Planning

Upright: looking ahead, expansion, rapid growth,

Reversed: obstacles, delays, frustration

In Love:Kissing

52. Have faith that the changes you're considering or experiencing are for the best.

53 Four of Wands- Marriage or Engagement

Upright: community, home, celebration,

Reversed: lack of support, transience, home conflicts

In Love:Playing

53. The ascended masters are helping you change your life in positive ways. Ask for their help with any aspect of these situations, such as additional ideas, opportunities, courage, and so forth.

54 Five of Wands- Conflict

Upright: competition, rivalry, conflict,

Reversed: avoiding conflict, respecting differences

In Love: Watching

54. The angels are guiding and supporting you as you make healthy and necessary changes in your life.

55 Six of Wands- Success

Upright: victory, success, public reward,

Reversed: excess pride, lack of recognition, punishment

In Love: Touching

55. This is a period of "out with the old, in with the new." Welcome these changes, as they bring about new blessings.

56 Seven of Wands- Control

Upright: perseverance, defensive, maintaining control,

Reversed: give up, destroyed confidence, overwhelmed

In Love: Whispering

56. As you go through changes with your home life, career, and relationships, stay focused on your inner spirit's growth. Find the blessing within each change you're experiencing.

57 Eight of Wands-Movement

Upright: rapid action, movement, quick decisions,

Reversed: panic, waiting, slowdown

In Love:Savoring

57. The changes you are experiencing are for the best. Trust these changes to lead you where you want to go.

58 Nine of Wands- Standing your Ground

Upright: resilience, grit, last stand or try

Reversed: exhaustion, fatigue, questioning motivations

In Love:Caressing

58. Your finances are improving, and there will be a positive change in your financial flow. This could also signal a job promotion or career change, with an increased salary.

59 Ten of Wands- Responsibility

Upright: accomplishment, responsibility, burden,

Reversed: inability to delegate, overstressed, burnt out

In Love:Penetrating

59. The changes you are going through are bringing you closer to your Divine life purpose. You can calm anxieties by spending time on activities related to your spiritual interests.

60 Page of Wands- Exciting News

Upright: exploration, excitement, freedom,

Reversed: lack of direction, procrastination, creating conflict

In Love:Abandon

60. You are vacillating between focusing upon Spirit and the material world. This number is a call for you to balance your focus, and always remember that Spirit is your source and the force behind everything in your life.

61 Knight of Wands- Take Action

Upright: action, adventure, fearlessness,

Reversed: anger, impulsiveness, recklessness

In Love:Embracing

61. Keep your thoughts about your material life (such as home, work, body, and possessions) very positively focused. Your thoughts are affecting your life, so only think about your desires and not about any fears.

62 Queen of Wands- Stay Strong

Upright: courage, determination, joy,

Reversed: selfishness, jealousy, insecurities

In Love: Undressing

62. Keep believing that the details of your life are working out in miraculous ways. Your faith opens the door for miracles!

63 King of Wands - Leap of faith

Upright: big picture, leader, overcoming challenges,

Reversed: impulsive, overbearing, unachievable expectations

In Love:Embracing Closely

63. The ascended masters are helping you with the daily aspects of your life. Ask them for help, and then be open to receiving the assistance that they bring to you in the form of ideas, guidance, and unexpected gifts.

Water & Emotions

Water is emotional and psychic energy. It's passive/receptive/yin. The emotional connection needed for a woman to get wet is found among these cards.

The Water Signs:

Cancer, Scorpio Pisces

Intuitive, emotional and ultra-sensitive, water signs can be as mysterious as the ocean itself. Like water, they can be refreshing, or they can drown you in their depths. These signs often have intense dreams and borderline-psychic intuition. Security is important to them—after all, water needs a container, or it dries up and disappears.

64 *Ace of Cups- Intuition & Instinct*

Upright: new feelings, spirituality, intuition,

Reversed: Emotional loss, blocked creativity, emptiness

In Love:Ecstasy

64. You are fully supported by the angels in every area of your life. Give any fears or worries to the angels, and ask them for any assistance that you need right now.

65 Two of Cups- Connection

Upright: unity, partnership, connection,

Reversed: imbalance, broken communication, tension

In Love:Involvement

65. Congratulations on the positive changes you're making in your life right now. This is an excellent time to make changes at home, work, or within relationships. Follow your inner truth.

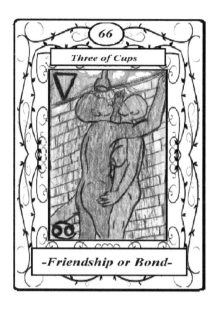

66 Three of Cups- Friendship or Bond

Upright: friendship, community, happiness,

Reversed: overindulgence, gossip, isolation

In Love:Passion

66. When you're burdened by worries, stress, or fear, it's more difficult to hear your angels' loving help. This is a message for you to spend time in prayer and meditation. Ask for spiritual intervention, and open your arms to receive the help that always follows prayers.

67 Four of Cups-Thinking vs Feeling

Upright: apathy contemplation, disconnectedness,

Reversed: sudden awareness, choosing happiness, acceptance

In Love:Habit

67. Well done! You're on the right path at home and at work.

68 Five of Cups- Negative Energy

Upright: loss, grief, self-pity,

Reversed: acceptance, moving on, finding peace

In Love:Guilt

68. Remember that Spirit is the source of your income. Worry doesn't assist you with your finances, but prayer always helps every part of your life.

69 Six of Cups- Healing Self or Others

Upright: familiarity, happy memories, healing,

Reversed: moving forward, leaving home, independence

In Love: Memory

69. As you spend time working on activities related to your spiritual passions and interests, every part of your life automatically improves.

70 Seven of Cups-Positive Energy

Upright: searching for purpose, choices, daydreaming,

Reversed: lack of purpose, diversion, confusion

In Love:Flights of Fancy

70. This is a message from God that you're on the right path. Keep up the good work!

71 Eight of Cups- Lessons Learned

Upright: walking away, disillusionment, leaving behind,

Reversed: avoidance, fear of change, fear of loss

In Love:Bashfulness

71. You are on track with your desires and manifestations. Just stay positive and optimistic, and all of your dreams will be right there for you.

72 Nine of Cups- Stability

Upright: satisfaction, emotional stability, luxury,

Reversed: lack of inner joy, smugness, dissatisfaction

In Love:Euphoria

72. Have faith that you're taking the right steps toward the manifestation of your desires
... because you are!

73 Ten of Cups- Leveling Up

Upright: inner happiness, fulfillment, dreams coming true,

Reversed: shattered dreams, broken family, domestic disharmony

In Love:Attachment

73. The ascended masters are guiding you, and you are listening to them accurately. Stay on your present path, as it is illuminated with blessings and gifts.

74 Page of Cups- A Surprise

Upright: happy surprise, dreamer, sensitivity,

Reversed: emotional immaturity, insecurity, disappointment

In Love:Jealousy

74. The angels surround you and walk beside you every step of the way. You're on the fast track to the manifestation of your dreams, so stick to the ideas and activities you're involved with now.

75 Knight of Cups- Romance

Upright: following the heart, idealist, romantic,

Reversed: moodiness, disappointment

In Love: Modesty

75. The changes you're making or considering are exactly right for you.

76 Queen of Cups- Seek and or give Comfort

Upright: compassion, calm, comfort,

Reversed: martyrdom, insecurity, dependence

In Love:Tenderness

76. You're on the right path, and your material needs are fully supported by your choices and actions.

77 King of Cups- Balance

Upright: compassion, control, balance,

Reversed: coldness, moodiness, bad advice

In Love:Satisfaction

77. Keep up the great work! Everything you're doing right now has the Midas touch!

1. (Aces) Action, new beginnings and opportunities, gifts, initiative, originality

2. Duality, polarity, diplomacy, choices, cooperation, partnerships, tension

3. Fertility, flirtation, creativity, enthusiasm, optimism, imagination

4. Power, stability, organisation, management, efficiency, concentration

5. Flexibility, freedom-loving, highly sexed, innovative, adventurous, changeable

6. Trust, beauty, domestic, supportive, pride, problem-solving, responsible

7. Analytical, clever, research, solitude, understanding, meditation, mysticism

8. Strength, power, skill, determination, hard-working, passionate

9. Idealistic, teacher, intuitive, generous, dedication, devotion, visionary

10. The culmination and 'seeding' of the energy of each individual suit, legacy, endings that lead to new beginnings

2-4 are cardinal – (enterprise)

5-7 are fixed – (stability)

8-10 are mutable – (adaptability)

Capricorn Zodiac Sign

The Goat

December 22 - January 19

Earth

Cardinal

Fire of Earth

Mountains & Streams

The Devil

2,3 & 4 of Pentacles

Capricorn are talented at applying their deep intelligence & ambition to external & internal matters. Viewing the spider web of life with unique eyes. Stability and order are important to them as this makes them good organizers, planners and Strategists. Their goals are often lofty, and they achieve them slowly but purposefully, and systematically with precision. They are gifted with a sharp intuition and Tongue. They can be rather secretive about what they perceive and have a habit of rumination in all aspects of life. They are patient with themselves but also harsh and self blame. They have confidence that they can accomplish all their goals if they follow their step-by-step plan or because of their skills. They are responsible people that often take the heavy burden of others both willingly or not, or just because they are so capable and don't like asking for help. However, they find it difficult to share their own troubles and can struggle with depression if they don't learn how to express their feelings. They also embrace the Chaos of life and seek Universal understanding.

Aquarius Zodiac Sign

The Water Bearer

January 20 - February 18

Air

Fixed

Air of Air

Clouds & Sky

The Star

5,6 & 7 of Swords

Aquarius more often than not comes off as an oddball, weird, strange and different to the normal standard. They have quirky and unique personalities and quietly to go about accomplishing their goals in quiet, and unorthodox ways. Oftentimes, just because they choose to take the path less worn path, the results of their eccentric methods are surprisingly effective. They are the humanitarians, often taking up for the greater good of humanity, Friends and Family and any cause that touches them. Many of them are also easy going and their peculiarity and unique outlook on life alongside their curious nature makes them fast friendships of a very loyal person. Sometimes, if they don't strive to motivate themselves, they can succumb to laziness or feeling a lack of direction. Many are often gifted with a strong sense of art and poetry and are more in tune with others feelings.

Pisces Zodiac Sign

The Fish

February 19 - March 20

Water

Mutable

Water of Water

Pools of Water

The Moon

8, 9 & 10 of Cups

Pisces are the dreamers and mystics and creators of unique but you may never know that as they seem outwardly calm and collected. Many of them have extremely vivid inner lives and ideas filled with fantasy, magic and wonder. They may find it hard to express that inner life, meaning that many of them are introverts and tend to avoid crowds and to many friends or crowded places. They are honest, compassionate, and trustworthy but they can sometimes take it too far and be rather gullible and because of that they can be taken advantage of easily and may not even realize it. Beneath their quiet exterior, Pisces has an intense determination, which helps them transcend and overcome any obstacles that come their way pushing through to the finish line or end. The immense Determination and willpower to complete any task, and can make them have a deep impact on others lives and goals.

Aries Zodiac Sign

The Ram

March 21 - April 19

Fire

Cardinal

Fire of Fire

Lightning

The Emperor

2, 3 & 4 of Wands

Aries sign often have an exciting and enthusiastic energy and life force and personality. They often seek new and challenging adventures that can push their limits. They are driven, ambitious, curious, stubborn and tend to have a strong sense of justice and moral code and an excess of energy. They love competition, in all its forms. They are generally quite optimistic, and they love being placed in leadership positions and being in charge and in the spotlight. They are Leaders and people of strategy who can accomplish almost anything when they put there mind to it. They are also very protective and over reactive. They however tend to be more willing to fight and stand up for their beliefs and are a fierce enemy. Prone to fits of anger or self blame when things go badly or not in their favor.

Taurus Zodiac Sign

The Bull

April 20 - May 20

Earth

Fixed

Air of Earth

Plains

The Hierophant

5, 6 & 7 of Pentacles

Taurus signs are often incredibly dedicated, reliable and dependable if they feel you or a cause is worthy. Above all, they value their sense of security and stability and will be greedy with it. Taurus will plan and follows through if its worth their time. They tend to be rather stubborn and dislike change or when others exhibit a differing opinion. When they settle with a routine that they like, it can take much effort to get them to change. They can be emotional and tend to cling to things familiar to them. Prone to the pot and kettle situation they cause and may even enjoy Drama and can be bitter if they feel wronged. They can also be loyal and stubborn in all things and are very opinionated. Love and finding it tend to be a focus. They also have difficulty in equal give and take.

Gemini Zodiac Sign

The Twins

May 21 - June 20

Air

Mutable

Water of Air

Vibrations

The Lovers

8, 9 & 10 of Swords

Gemini signs often enjoy socializing and love surrounding themselves with people and are the life of the party, the social butterfly. They are ruled by the planet Mercury. So they are never happier or more in their element than when they are sharing their ideas and communicating with the people around them, shopping, socializing and living life. They enjoy chit-chat & conversation and tend to have expression and communication very high on their list of life priorities and enjoying any and all the things they can. Sometimes their love for sharing themselves with others, and their never-ending list of ideas can make them seem nervous, excited, and sometimes even manic or hyper or all over the place. Often prone to falling in love too quick and deep they have difficulty balancing themselves at times and keeping themselves in check. They also have to remember to not burn themselves out taking on too much.

Cancer Zodiac Sign

The Crab

June 21 - July 22

Water

Cardinal

Fire of Water

Rain & Springs

The Chariot

2, 3 & 4 of Cups

Cancer needs to be needed and want to be wanted. They have a great inner desire to feel loved and appreciated in every part of their lives. They feel a need to be in the spotlight. Sometimes acting spoiled. This is needed so that they can develop a sense of security and identity of self. To the Cancer sign, their sense of home is very important to their feeling of safety and comfort and overall well being . They will strive for safety and comfort. They find it rather difficult to achieve peace unless they feel safe in their home or surroundings. They are talented at developing home environments for people that are close to them, in both an emotional ,physical & mental sense. They however can be selfish and feel owed by those around them. Cancer is also a nurturer and caregiver. Does well with children. Needs a purpose and dislikes stagnation but can be prone to it.

Leo Zodiac Sign

The Lion

July 23 - August 22

Fire

Fixed

Air of Fire

Sun & Deserts

Strength

5, 6 & 7 of Wands

Leos tend to have almost a James bond air about them. Their ruler is the Sun, and thus they are therefore talented at bringing warmth, Life and Energy to all they do. Bringing into life interactions of energy and light into the relationships that are important to them but can drain others when they are negative. Many Leos will have a large group of friends that adore them and seek to be near them. Drama is also a big part of their personality. They have a kind of natural charisma which often makes other signs gravitate towards them, causing the ego to develop as well as a need to feel important and wanted. Leos love to be at the center of attention and they deeply appreciate compliments and even flattery and when there in the spotlight. Their happy and outgoing attitude towards life makes them pleasurable to be around or tiring for long periods as other signs lack the Leos Energy.

Virgo Zodiac Sign

The Virgin

August 23 - September 22

Earth

Mutable

Water of Earth

Vast Fields

The Hermit

8, 9 & 10 of Pentacles

Virgo signs have very capable, organized and analytical minds, which often makes them a pleasure to talk with and brilliant at business and research. Even when they have rather fantastic stories, the charming way they tell them can make those stories convincing both in a good and bad way. Virgos are curious people, and they have a natural gift for research whether it comes to assignments, or even people they have a need and want to know. They also often have great memory and a talent for intuition allowing for great insight into life. They make for excellent team members in both work and social situations. They also have much compassion. They love to collaborate, although their sometimes critical nature can annoy others when those criticisms are not understood as they themselves have difficulty accepting criticism.

Libra Zodiac Sign

The Scales

September 23 - October 22

Air

Cardinal

Fire of Fire

Great Wind

Justice

2, 3 & 4 of Swords

The Libra thrives when their needs of balance, justice, and stability are met and on equal footing. They are charming and smooth individuals that somehow always surround themselves with a sense of beauty and harmony. Although some of them can go to extremes searching for that harmony, which can make their situations unreasonable or unhealthy when they obsess. Their ruling planet is Venus, meaning that they are very nurturing, caring, loyal and they can make great defenders of the downtrodden and causes close to there large hearts. They often thrive in a Family environments. Often sensitive and sometimes, can be shy if they find difficulties in coming out of their shell and letting their guard down or trusting. Despite their more introverted side they still love a good debate and chat. They make caring partners and mediators.

Scorpio Zodiac Sign

The Scorpion

October 23 - November 21

Water

Fixed

Air of Water

Vast Sea

Death

5, 6 & 7 of Cups

Scorpios are often misunderstood and deeply emotional people with deep insights and traits. They are quite bold, with intense personalities and feelings that hide underneath their cool and collected exterior. They come across as cold and aloof at times. They are capable people that can complete great and massive projects with control and confidence. Their intensity and intelligence when approaching a situation means that they can surmount almost all obstacles if they can truly put their mind to the task and not be their own worst enemy. Many Scorpios have an unshakable focus when they need to call on it. However, they are often secretive, seeming withdrawn and uninterested, when they are actually keenly observing. They also tend to pull away from those they love in times of great stress or hardships or loss. They love deeply and can be loyal to those they trust. But can be self-destructive and withdrawn & self blame when things don't go their way in life.

Sagittarius Zodiac Sign

The Centaur

November 22 - December 21

Fire

Mutable

Water of Fire

Rainbow & Reflection

Temperance

8, 9 & 10 of Wands

The Sagittarius more often than not will gain the reputation of the philosopher, Thinker and planner among their fellows. They have a great ability to focus, but this may be surprising since many of them love exploring and traveling the world and experiencing it, and seaseing the day and all it has to offer. They must learn how to channel their energy or else they risk stretching themselves out too thin going in too many directions. They often are hasty individuals and lack patience in many aspects of life. When they encounter failure they can sometimes make a sudden comeback, much to the surprise of others. While they are loyal friends, they may find it hard to commit as this can run counter to their desire for freedom and expansion. They seek life's mysteries and sights & understanding. They can also be seen as slackers or free spirits. Sometimes scaterd in their ability to focus, but deeply kind hearted.

-Lovers Quick Spread-

Start with a simple 6 card spread:

Card 1: What is my heart's desire?

Card 2: What is blocking me from fulfilling it?

Card 3: What is my deeper unconscious desire?

Card 4: What is preventing me from seeing this?

Card 5: How can I balance and integrate these desires?

Card 6: What can I do atain my fulfillment?

Optional-

*Card 7: What is the Universe trying to tell me?

To view and Download the Deck please Visit

https://chaos-tarot-spiritual-consultant.webnode.com/the-adult-lovers-shadow-tarot-oracle-printable-deck/

Please Email me at

Chaostarotspiritualconsulting@gmail.com

To get a full copy of the JPEG files for printing purposes otherwise you may use the link above to view and print the PNG images.

30	31	32	33
Nine of Pentacles	Ten of Pentacles	Page of Pentacles	Knight of Pentacles
-Rewards-	-Your Life-	-Desire & Dive-	-Responsibility-

34	35
Queen of Pentacles	King of Pentacles
-Security-	-Prosperity-

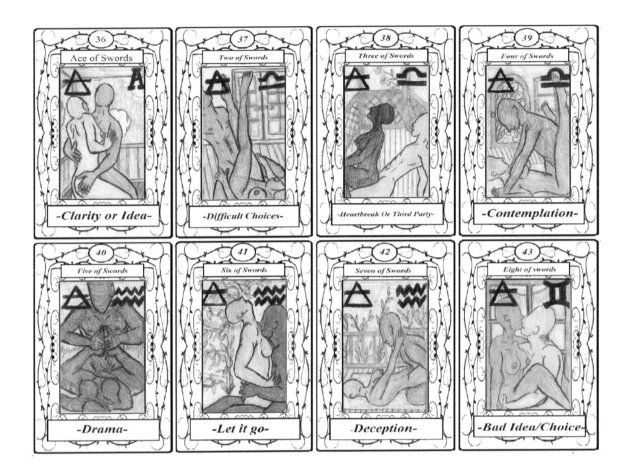

44	45	46	47
Nine of Swords	*Ten of Swords*	*Page of Swords*	*Knight of Swords*
-UnHappy-	-Loss or Feeling Loss-	-Unstable-	-Acting Without Thinking-

48	49		
Queen of Swords	*King of Swords*		
-Perception-	-Actions & Reactions-		

50	51	52	53
Ace of Wands	*Two of Wands*	*Three of Wands*	*Four of Wands*
-Manifestation-	*-Thinking Before Acting-*	**-Plans or Planning-**	*-Marriage or Engagement-*

54	55	56	57
Five of Wands	*Six of Wands*	*Seven of Wands*	*Eight of Wands*
-Conflict-	**-Success-**	**-Control-**	**-Movement-**